COUNTRY PROFILES

INDONESIA

BY CHRISTINA LEAF

BELLWETHER MEDIA • MINNEAPOLIS, MN

Blastoff! Discovery launches
a new mission: reading to learn.
Filled with facts and features, each
book offers you an exciting new
world to explore!

This edition first published in 2020 by Bellwether Media, Inc.

No part of this publication may be reproduced in whole or in part
without written permission of the publisher.
For information regarding permission, write to Bellwether Media, Inc.,
Attention: Permissions Department,
6012 Blue Circle Drive, Minnetonka, MN 55343.

Library of Congress Cataloging-in-Publication Data

Names: Leaf, Christina, author.
Title: Indonesia / by Christina Leaf.
Description: Minneapolis, MN : Bellwether Media, Inc., [2020] |
    Series: Blastoff! Discovery. Country Profiles | Includes bibliographical
    references and index. | Audience: Grades 3-8. | Audience:
    Ages 7-13.
Identifiers: LCCN 2019001509 (print) | LCCN 2019002724 (ebook)
    | ISBN 9781618915917 (electronic) | ISBN 9781644870501
    (hardcover)
Subjects: LCSH: Indonesia–Juvenile literature.
Classification: LCC DS615 (ebook) | LCC DS615 .L43 2020 (print)
    | DDC 959.8–dc23
LC record available at https://lccn.loc.gov/2019001509

Editor: Rebecca Sabelko   Designer: Brittany McIntosh

Printed in the United States of America, North Mankato, MN.

TABLE OF CONTENTS

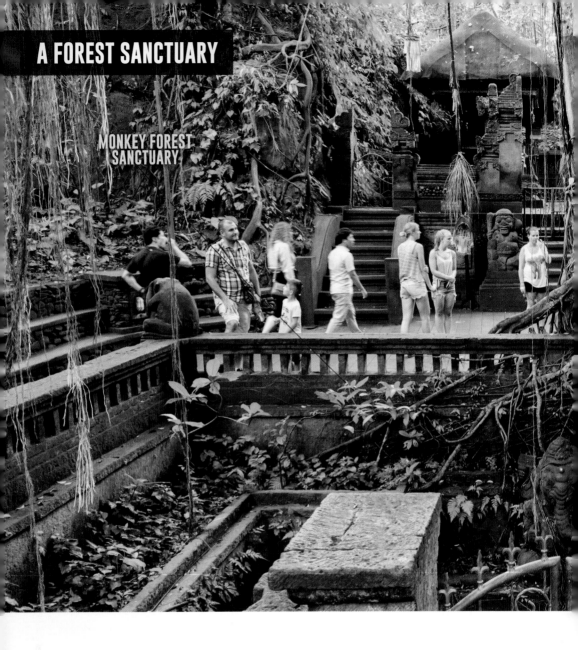

A FOREST SANCTUARY

MONKEY FOREST
SANCTUARY

A family wanders through the center of Ubud, on the island of Bali. Just outside of town is the famed Monkey Forest **Sanctuary**. There, gray long-tailed macaques play in the trees.

OTHER TOP SITES

BOROBUDUR TEMPLE

BUNAKEN NATIONAL MARINE PARK

LAKE TOBA

TANAH LOT

Leafy nutmeg trees draped with vines shade the forest path where the family walks. Scattered along the walkway are worn stone statues covered in moss. Macaques lounge in the trees above the visitors. Shortly into their walk, the family comes upon an old temple. Fanciful carvings cover the outside and roof. Indonesia hides many wonders in its forests!

LOCATION

A NEW CAPITAL?
In 2019, Indonesia announced plans to change its capital city.

MEDAN

MALAYSIA

BORNEO

SUMATRA

INDONESIA

JAKARTA

BANDUNG

SURABAYA

JAVA

INDIAN OCEAN

Indonesia is an island nation in Southeast Asia. Its 735,358 square miles (1,904,569 square kilometers) make it the largest country in the region. Indonesia consists of around 17,500 islands in the Indian and Pacific Oceans. The biggest are Sumatra, New Guinea, and Borneo. Indonesia's capital, Jakarta, lies in northeastern Java.

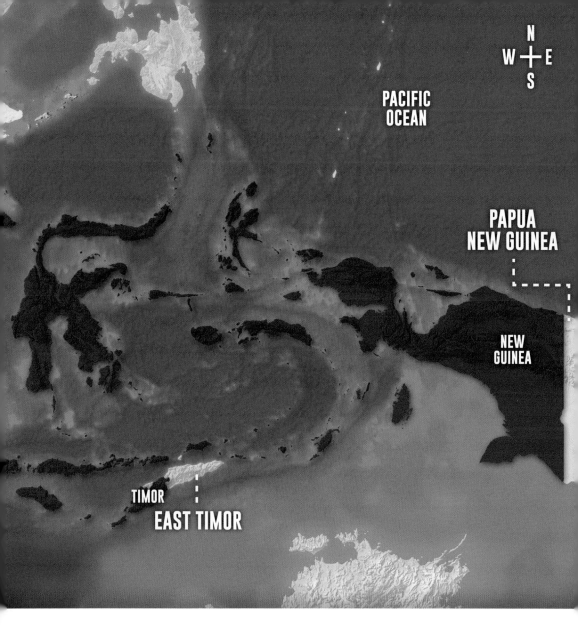

PACIFIC
OCEAN

N
W＋E
S

PAPUA
NEW GUINEA

NEW
GUINEA

TIMOR
EAST TIMOR

Several of Indonesia's islands share borders with other
countries. In the far east, Indonesia shares the island of
New Guinea with Papua New Guinea. West of New Guinea,
the island of Timor also includes the country of East Timor.
Indonesia shares the island of Borneo with Malaysia in
the north.

LANDSCAPE AND CLIMATE

Most of Indonesia's larger islands are similar in landscape. High mountains command the center of the islands. Many of these mountains are actually **volcanoes**, like the Barisan Mountains on Sumatra. Thick **rain forests** cover the mountains and surrounding areas. Short rivers flow down the mountains. Indonesia's longest, the Kapuas River, cuts through Borneo. Lowlands around the coasts are covered in swamps.

KAPUAS RIVER

N
W + E
S

= BARISAN MOUNTAINS

KRAKATOA

In 1883, the volcano Krakatoa erupted. It set off a giant wave which became one of the largest tsunamis in history. Little of the island it sat on remains today.

JAKARTA
Average seasonal highs and lows

JANUARY
HIGH: 86 °F (30 °C)
LOW: 79 °F (26 °C)

APRIL
HIGH: 90 °F (32 °C)
LOW: 79 °F (26 °C)

JULY
HIGH: 88 °F (31 °C)
LOW: 79 °F (26 °C)

OCTOBER
HIGH: 91 °F (33 °C)
LOW: 81 °F (27 °C)

°F = degrees Fahrenheit
°C = degrees Celsius

Indonesia is hot and sticky thanks to a **tropical** climate. Temperatures change little throughout the year because the country lies along the equator. Rain falls year-round. However, **monsoons** between December and March bring downpours.

The rain forests of Indonesia are brimming with wildlife. Many of these species are found only on these islands. Tigers hunt prey in the forests of Sumatra. There and on Borneo, orangutans swing through the trees. Elephants and rare rhinos are found on several of the country's islands. Peafowl strut through Java, and tiny tarsiers cling to trees on Sulawesi.

On southern islands, bandicoots search for insects to eat. Cockatoos and birds of paradise perch in the trees. Indonesia's national animal, the fierce komodo dragon, lounges on beaches and in forests.

SUMATRAN TIGER

SPECTRAL TARSIER

ASIAN ELEPHANT

FLASHY DANCES

Male birds of paradise put on quite a show for females. They perform fancy dances and flash bright feathers.

KOMODO
DRAGON

KOMODO DRAGON

Life Span: 30 years
Red List Status: vulnerable

komodo dragon range =

LEAST CONCERN	NEAR THREATENED	VULNERABLE	ENDANGERED	CRITICALLY ENDANGERED	EXTINCT IN THE WILD	EXTINCT

A TOP POPULATION
Indonesia's population is the fourth largest in the world!

Indonesia is one of the most **diverse** countries in the world. Its nearly 263 million people belong to more than 300 different **ethnic** groups. The largest is the Javanese. They live on Java and make up two of every five Indonesian people. The Sundanese and the Malay are the next largest groups.

Because there are so many different **cultures**, Indonesia is home to many different languages. Most people learn their **native** language at home. The official language, Bahasa Indonesia, is taught in schools. Almost all Indonesians are Muslim. Some people in the country practice Christianity or Buddhism.

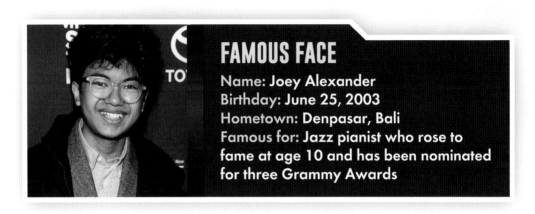

FAMOUS FACE

Name: Joey Alexander
Birthday: June 25, 2003
Hometown: Denpasar, Bali
Famous for: Jazz pianist who rose to fame at age 10 and has been nominated for three Grammy Awards

SPEAK BAHASA INDONESIA

ENGLISH	BAHASA INDONESIA	HOW TO SAY IT
hello	salam	sah-LAHM
goodbye	selamat tinggal	seh-LA-mat TEEN-gahl
please	tolong	TOE-lowng
thank you	terima kasih	ta-REE-mah CAH-see
yes	ya	YAH
no	tidak	TEE-dahk

BALI

COMMUNITIES

Rural areas are home to nearly half of Indonesia's people. Many of the people who live in these small villages are farmers. Villages vary widely between islands and ethnic groups. Homes may look different from place to place, as do community structures. However, throughout Indonesia, the village community holds importance second only to family.

ISLAND OF SULAWESI

Indonesians who live in cities often live in houses or apartments like those in Europe and the United States. Some Indonesians live in shacks on city outskirts. On islands, people take buses, **mopeds**, or cars to get around. Boats or planes take people to neighboring islands.

Indonesia is rich with **traditions**. Customs vary between islands and people groups. On most islands, people greet everyone with a smile. Especially in smaller villages, people are friendly and chatty, even with strangers.

Dance is an important part of Indonesian culture, especially on Java and Bali. It is most important in theatrical performances. In these, brightly costumed dancers tell stories through movement. Dance can also be a key part of religious ceremonies, or just a way to have fun!

JAVA

FIGHTING OR DANCING?

Some Indonesian dances are inspired by martial arts! Rhythmic music accompanies martial arts performances. These martial arts have inspired some Sundanese dances.

Children in Indonesia attend elementary and secondary school from ages 7 to 15. Some go on to more secondary school and even university. However, children attending rural schools often struggle. Schools may lack good teachers or students may be needed at home. Recently, the government has made education a key focus.

About half of Indonesia's workers have **service jobs**. Many work in hotels and restaurants that serve Indonesia's millions of **tourists**. Other Indonesians are farmers and fishers. Large **plantations** grow cocoa, coffee beans, and coconuts. Smaller farms grow rice and bananas. Factory workers make cement, rubber and wood products, and electronics.

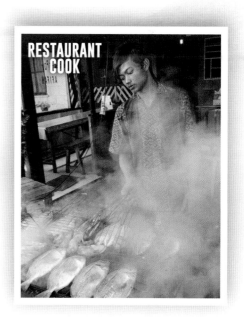

RESTAURANT COOK

RICE FARMERS

PENCAK
SILAT

Many traditional sports are popular in Indonesia. *Pencak silat* and *sisemba* are favorite **martial arts**. People enjoy bull racing on the island of Madura. Indonesians are excellent at badminton and have won several Olympic medals in the sport. Soccer is another favorite activity. Indonesia's clear waters offer fabulous surfing and **snorkeling**.

SNORKELING

On a day-to-day basis, Indonesians enjoy watching movies and television. A night out might include a puppet show. Sundanese shows are usually performed with wooden puppets, while shadow puppets are common on Java and Bali.

THE LATE SHOW

Puppet shows in Java may last all night!

BATIK FABRIC

Indonesia is famous for this method of dying fabric.

What You Need:
- blue gel glue
- white fabric
- liquid acrylic paint
- paint brushes
- scrub brush
- wax paper

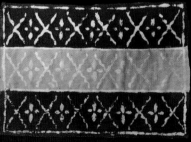

Instructions:
1. Lay the fabric on the wax paper. Use the glue to draw a design on the fabric. Let dry for several hours or overnight.
2. Paint over the fabric and glue. Let the paint dry.
3. Soak the fabric in warm water for one hour.
4. Scrub off the glue and let the fabric dry again.

FOOD

FIVE FAVORITES

Indonesia has five national dishes. Along with nasi goreng, rendang, satay, and gado-gado, a soup called *soto ayam* takes top honor.

Rice is everywhere in Indonesia. People eat it with spices or with a main dish, such as fish, meat, or vegetables. Fried rice called *nasi goreng* is found across all the islands. *Nasi uduk* is another favorite. This rice is cooked in coconut milk.

Favorite meats include water buffalo and chicken. *Rendang* is a famous dish of curried meat. *Satay*, or skewers of meat dipped in peanut sauce, are popular street foods. Peanut sauce covers veggies in another favorite food called *gado-gado*. Many Indonesian desserts include coconut milk or fresh fruit.

RENDANG

GADO-GADO

AVOCADO MILKSHAKE

Avocadoes are often found in desserts in Indonesia. Have an adult help you make this sweet treat!

Ingredients:

1 ripe avocado

1 cup milk

3 tablespoons sweetened condensed milk

1/2 cup ice cubes

chocolate syrup (optional)

Steps:

1. Cut the avocado in half and scoop out the insides, removing the pit.

2. Add the avocado to a blender with the milk, sweetened condensed milk, and ice cubes. Blend until smooth and foamy.

3. Add chocolate syrup to taste and enjoy!

CELEBRATIONS

Many of Indonesia's holidays are connected to religion. Muslims celebrate the end of a month of **fasting** on *Lebaran*. People travel to visit families and celebrate with feasts and prayers. In March, Hindus on Bali observe a day of silence on *Nyepi*, or Hindu New Year.

NYEPI

GREBEG SUDIRO

Other festivals celebrate Indonesia's cultures. *Grebeg Sudiro* in January honors the Chinese New Year on Java with colorful parades. During June's Sentani Lake festival, brightly costumed dancers perform on a boat to celebrate the culture of Papua. Everyone enjoys Independence Day in August. People hold contests and play games. They come together to celebrate their country!

TIMELINE

1942
Japan invades the country during World War II

1670
The Dutch gain control of the whole of Indonesia, known as the Dutch East Indies until 1949

1967
General Suharto begins his 30-year rule, during which he stabilizes Indonesia through military force

1949
Indonesia becomes an independent country after four years of war

1883
The volcano Krakatoa erupts and causes a massive tsunami

1969
West Papua, or New Guinea, becomes a part of Indonesia

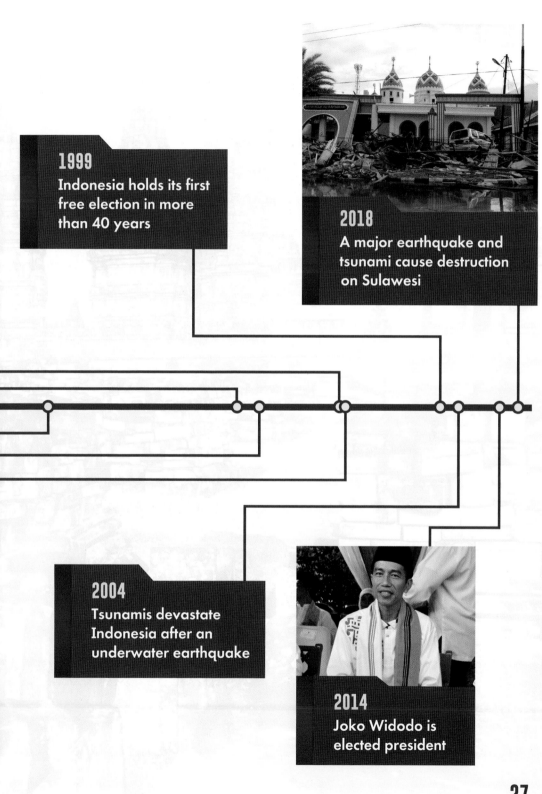

1999
Indonesia holds its first free election in more than 40 years

2018
A major earthquake and tsunami cause destruction on Sulawesi

2004
Tsunamis devastate Indonesia after an underwater earthquake

2014
Joko Widodo is elected president

INDONESIA FACTS

Official Name: Republic of Indonesia

Flag of Indonesia: Indonesia's flag is divided into two colors. The top half is red for courage, and the bottom is white for honesty. The flag has been used since the 13th century in various ways. It was officially adopted by the country in 1945.

Area: 735,358 square miles
(1,904,569 square kilometers)

Capital City: Jakarta

Important Cities: Bekasi, Surabaya, Bandung, Medan, Tangerang

Population:
262,787,403 (July 2018)

WHERE PEOPLE LIVE

COUNTRYSIDE
44.7%

CITY
55.3%

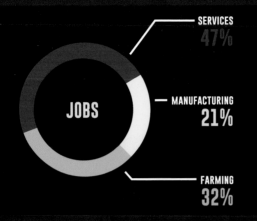

JOBS

SERVICES
47%

MANUFACTURING
21%

FARMING
32%

Main Exports:

palm oil

rubber

electrical
machinery

machinery
parts

National Holiday:
Independence Day (August 17)

Main Language:
Bahasa Indonesia

Form of Government:
presidential republic

Title for Country Leader:
president

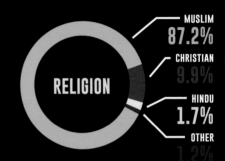

RELIGION

MUSLIM
87.2%

CHRISTIAN
9.9%

HINDU
1.7%

OTHER
1.2%

Unit of Money:
Indonesian rupiah

GLOSSARY

cultures—beliefs, arts, and ways of life in places or societies

diverse—made up of people or things that are different from one another

ethnic—related to a group of people who share customs and an identity

fasting—choosing not to eat all food or particular foods for a time

martial arts—styles and techniques of fighting and self-defense that are practiced as sport

monsoons—winds that shift direction each season; monsoons bring heavy rain.

mopeds—small motorbikes

native—originally from the area or related to a group of people that began in the area

plantations—large farms that grow coffee beans, cotton, rubber, or other crops; plantations are mainly found in warm climates.

rain forests—thick, green forests that receive a lot of rain

rural—related to the countryside

sanctuary—a place of protection

service jobs—jobs that perform tasks for people or businesses

snorkeling—swimming underwater while breathing through a tube

tourists—people who travel to visit another place

traditions—customs, ideas, or beliefs handed down from one generation to the next

tropical—part of the tropics; the tropics is a hot, rainy region near the equator.

volcanoes—holes in the earth; when a volcano erupts, hot ash, gas, or melted rock called lava shoots out.

TO LEARN MORE

AT THE LIBRARY

Hibbs, Linda. *All About Indonesia: Stories, Songs, and Crafts for Kids.* North Clarendon, Vt.: Tuttle Pub., 2014.

Nagara, Innosanto. *My Night in the Planetarium.* New York, N.Y.: Seven Stories Press, 2016.

Wiseman, Blaine. *Indonesia.* New York, N.Y.: AV2 by Weigl, 2017.

ON THE WEB

FACTSURFER

Factsurfer.com gives you a safe, fun way to find more information.

1. Go to www.factsurfer.com.

2. Enter "Indonesia" into the search box and click 🔍.

3. Select your book cover to see a list of related web sites.

INDEX